*My love and thanks to Maude Meehan
and Judy Greenan for their editorial
wisdom, and to Barbara Lawlor for
guiding me through the wildflowers.*

I know there lives inside of me
a spirit of joy, incredibly free.

I feel it often. I'm blessed that it's there
whenever my life seems filled with despair.

When winds of injustice toss me around,
I look to the spirit, where calming is found.

> *It shows me a sunset, a rich golden glow,*
> *soothing my senses, helping me know*
> *that injustice, conflict, joy as well,*
> *are part of living, stories to tell*
> *of the life that is mine -*
>
> *my personal trial.*

Lessons in growth to be learned with a smile.

I've wandered through life
        with an ache in my heart,
        longing for someone
        to care for the part
        that's causing the pain,

whisk me away
    to a place where heartache
        has nowhere to stay.

A fairytale picture I learned as a child
    taught me unfairly,
        my vision beguiled
        by untruths of a world
        where I would be fine,
        for a knight on a charger
        would make life sublime.

Finally the spirit has taught me to see
    that the care my heart needs

        is found within me.

"But, where is this spirit?" so often I ask,
   making the search such a difficult task.

      I stumble around
         trying to find
            light in the darkness.

            Am I really that blind?

The spirit's right here,
   to be called on at will.

I don't have to struggle.

      I need to be still,
         feel its presence inside of me,

            lighting my darkness,

               setting me free.

Sometimes I put on a silly hat,
stand on my head or dance with the cat.

You know what happens when I act this way?
My joyful child comes out to play.

> *Why do I have to be silly to see*
> *that a playful child is*
> > *alive in me.*

Needing approval keeps it inside.
My critical adult will cause it to hide.

Critical adult and ego are one.
Letting go of both is the way to have fun.

When I flow with the spirit I'm perfectly clear
> *that my playful child*
> > *has nothing to fear.*

I wish I could loosen up,
                    allow myself fun,
take off my clothes
                    in the noonday sun,
prance in the warm rays,
                    feeling so free,

          tumble and roll with frivolity.

What do I do when I ought to let go?

I control myself.

          Well, I want you to know
              I'm tired of suppressing
                  the spirit inside.

New courage tells me ...

          Let go of false pride.

Often I search
    for words that are bright,
        to make me amazing
            in everyone's sight.

I want them to like me,

        whoever they are.

I'll do what I must to be a star.

        Isn't that crazy -
        giving ego control?

        I've submerged the spirit.
        I'm drowning my soul!

How dare I forget
    that the star that is me
        shines through my soul
        for people to see.

Words to impress are ego controlled.
As I speak from the spirit I feel love unfold.

At times I wonder why I feel
I'm so important
my work a big deal.

My work is nothing more, you see,
than what I do,
not what I be.

The way I be I keep inside,
the part of me I try to hide.

What I want to display for you
is a confident person -
powerful too.

Why don't I get it -
you're not blind,
you see the farce.

I need to be kind,
know I'm okay,
let the spirit take fears away.

Revealing my flaws,
being vulnerable too,
is how I will learn
to be honest with you.

9

"Put a smile on your face," my dad said to me.
"If you can't be happy, don't you see
we don't want you around. Go to your room!
Seeing you sad fills us with gloom."

As I grew up, what did I believe?
If I didn't act happy my friends would leave.

So I pretended a smile,
yet all the while
resenting the wrinkles
that started to pile.

Inhibited pain lined my eyes and my cheeks.
Smile lines, they called them. Isn't she sleek!

She seems to slide so lightly through life -
always smiling - as if her world has no strife.

Awareness of love from the spirit within
has come to assure me I don't need to grin.

Now as I share the way that I feel,
the scars of pretending are beginning to heal.

Yet, sometimes I rise and what do I say?
"I'm not in the mood to share today!"

> *How do I respond to myself at these times?*
> *"What an <u>awful</u> person you are," defines*
> *the way my thoughts are inclined to be.*

So how is my day?
>>> *Well, wait and see.*

My day is depressing -
> *no one else to accuse.*

>> *It's simply that way*
>>> *from the words that I use.*

The spirit inside has kind words to say.

"I love you in spite of your mood today."

> *If I hear the spirit, what happens to me?*

> *My critical self soon ceases to be.*

When there is something I need to know,
    I take myself and quickly go
        right to my desk where paper awaits.

    I lift my pen that by itself states
        so many things I need to know.

    Words appear in a constant flow.

There's a message for me
             if I'm ready to hear it.

I know in my heart it's a gift of the spirit.

I look at pictures of people I know,
            posing themselves
                        in a way that will show
                                    they're in control,
            wearing a smile -
                        perfectly preened.

            But inside all the while
                        they're hiding the pain
                                    they don't want you to see.

I know this is true - it used to be me.

Now I have a new life sense.

            It's not in my pose.
                        It won't show on my hair,
                                    or even my clothes.

I wish you could see it in photos of me,
            for its presence has clearly
                        set my life free.

I don't feel unique,
            or claim something new.

It's simply the spirit in me breaking through.

I gaze in the mirror,
*　　explore the lines,*
*　　　　feel sad and distressed*
*　　　　　　as I see time defined.*

Annoyed with myself
*　　　　by the signs that I see,*
*　　　　I nibble junk food*
*　　　　　　to satisfy me.*

Then I worry about pounds of fat,
*　　　　pads of flesh*
*　　　　on the seat where I sat.*

*　　　　Even my hands have turned on me.*
*　　　　My withered Grandma in them I see.*

I could worry for hours,
*　　　　but at last I'm aware*
*　　　　that dwelling on looks*
*　　　　　　is not worth the care.*

Flesh is adornment, along for the ride.
The essence of me is the spirit inside.

When I lie in my bed trapped by despair,
painful memories that seem so unfair
haunt the silence, invading the room
with tormented images
shrouded in gloom.

How do I get this torment
to cease?

I turn to the spirit
to bring me release.

In trust I take memories
that seem so unkind,
replace them with blessings
where quickly I find
a new sense of freedom
relief from the strife -

Spirit, not ego, brings joy to my life.

If I should decide to go away,
treat myself to a holiday,
please don't bother to ask me where.
for I'll only know when I get there.

"But you must have a plan," I say to me.
"That's the way you are, don't you agree!"

Not anymore. I'll enjoy this ride.
I'll trust the spirit to be my guide.
It knows where to go and what to do.
My bossy ego, I won't listen to you.

The control you assert is merely a test.
Give me a break. Go take a rest!

Why do I always seem to forget
that life is so short.

Why live in the future
when present is prime,

let concerns for tomorrow
consume all my time.

The answer is easy.
I've been ego controlled,
anxious for riches,
things bought and sold.

The present has simply seemed to be
a diving board
ready to catapult me
into the good life -

TOMORROW'S BEEN MY DREAM!

Have I lost my perspective?

That's the way it would seem.

Spirit alerts the ego in me
that this moment, the present,

is ALL there may be.

Trudging along a moon drenched road
 resentful and pained
  by the weight of my load,

I feel as if there's no respite in sight
 from all of the burdens filling my night.

Suddenly the full moon lights a new path,
 making it clear that the source of my wrath
  has come from inside me
   where I've chosen to be
    with burdensome thoughts
     that are angering me.

I feel myself warmed
 by this blanket of light
  that kindles my soul
   in the cold of the night.

Now, kind, loving thoughts
 turn my trudge to a glide.

At one with the spirit I feel peace inside.

There's something
    about the light in the dark
        that brings me perspective ·
           the shadows so stark.

The power in such beauty
    envelops my life,
        reminding me that ego
           is causing me strife.

As I gaze at the moon,
    my ego is zapped,
        freeing the spirit

        that before had seemed trapped.

The burdens of living
    that I carried all day
    are simply lifted,
        transported away.

The moonbeams ignite
    the light in my soul.

The spirit reminds me -
        Love is my goal.

Other books by Peggy Warren:

Very Much A Woman's Book

ME BOOKS: Where Love Starts
Where Love Goes
Where Love Is

A Visit With Myself